C000174325

PR$FITABLE *PRACTICE*

**A 90-DAY
KICKSTART PLAN FOR
PHYSIATRISTS**

PR$FITABLE
PRACTICE

A 90-DAY
**KICKSTART PLAN FOR
PHYSIATRISTS**

DR. HASSAN AKINBIYI

purposely
created
PUBLISHING

PROFITABLE PRACTICE
Published by Purposely Created Publishing Group™
Copyright © 2020 Hassan Akinbiyi
All rights reserved.

No part of this book may be reproduced, distributed or transmitted in any form by any means, graphic, electronic, or mechanical, including photocopy, recording, taping, or by any information storage or retrieval system, without permission in writing from the publisher, except in the case of reprints in the context of reviews, quotes, or references.

Printed in the United States of America

ISBN: 978-1-64484-154-9

Special discounts are available on bulk quantity purchases by book clubs, associations and special interest groups. For details email: sales@publishyourgift. com or call (888) 949-6228.

For information log on to www.PublishYourGift.com

To Yekinni Akinbiyi for your inspiration and love. You served as a role model, stressing the importance of hard work and education. Thank you for your tough love and discipline.

To Gladys Akinbiyi for being my rock, sticking with me when others gave up on me, for showing me love each and every day of my life. Thank you for showing me what it means to be strong and kind, for showing me what love is, and for being my inspiration.

This book is a tool for new attendings in their first one to five years, serving to help them build a profitable, independent practice, maximize revenue, and obtain financial independence and security.

TABLE OF CONTENTS

INTRODUCTION

I grew up in Chicago, Illinois, the youngest of my father's six kids. At a young age, I realized my calling to become a doctor. I was always fascinated by the inner workings of the mind and body. I began to study the human body. I performed well academically in high school, medical school, and residency. After completing residency, I started my own independent physiatry practice and soon built it into seven-figure revenue. I travelled the world, visiting many countries I always dreamed of visiting, including Brazil for Carnival, Dubai to bring in the New Year, and Sydney, Australia to watch the fireworks at the Sydney Opera House. I was also able to pay off the mortgage on my parents' home. After my father suffered his second of three strokes and before he eventually passed away, I was able to fly him to my Rehabilitation Hospital in Arizona to receive care as opposed to allowing the hospital to send him to a nursing home.

Despite all of this, I had an embarrassing secret. During my first year of college, my family was evicted from the home I spent all of my life in up to that point. We were now homeless and on the verge of being on the street. I vividly remember the sheriff coming to the house knocking on the door. It seemed like every other day. There was no warning. When I answered the door, he immediately dropped the bomb on me and let us know we needed to be out of the house within hours. My heart dropped, and I dropped to the floor and cried like a baby with a broken heart. I was numb and in a stupor for months. I had lost my home and my way. I no longer had a sense of certainty or any roots.

Because of this...NOW, I am dedicated to coaching new attendings on how to build lucrative, independent medical practices, so that they have financial independence, security, and the ability to plan and save for retirement. I want to make sure no one else has to experience that pain and embarrassment. I want you to achieve financial freedom, so you control your destiny.

CHAPTER 1

BUSINESS ENTITY

One of the most important steps prior to creating your entity is picking a name. The name of your business is the jumping off point for everything else and should justly represent your business. You must determine if the name already exists or if the name has already been trademarked or is currently in use. Once you have settled on a name, you must then form the business entity by filing the appropriate paperwork with the state agency that handles business filings. You can complete the paperwork yourself or with the assistance of a lawyer. You will need to apply for a federal tax ID number. Obtain a medical license in the state in which you plan to form your entity.

One of the most important factors to consider when forming your business entity is the tax implications that come along with its formation. Some of this is determined by the state in which you wish to create your entity. Each entity carries its own set of tax considerations, which may impact the amount of revenue you keep versus the amount you pay to the government. Other important things to consider include future growth of your business and how the type of entity you have formed can impact growth. You must also consider how and if you can pass the entity on to your heirs.

As you contemplate which entity to form, you must also consider the legal implications associated with the formation of your entity. Each entity carries its own amount of risk. Some entities place personal assets more at risk than others. The goal of any entity formed should be to minimize as much personal risk as possible. Avoiding exposure to your personal assets is of utmost importance.

The entity you form has an impact on your re-tirement planning. The entity created can impact the amount of revenue you generate and thus impact how much money you have available to fund your retirement accounts. The entity that minimizes the amount of taxes owed while providing the most coverage to your personal assets is the ideal scenario. The type of entity formed will determine if shareholders are owed stake. The type of entity can also impact estate planning

Each state has its own incorporation requirements and entity options available to you. Most states will require an article of incorporation. The state will need to establish strength of connection between the new entity and the state it is forming within. Some entities in one state may not be available for another state. It is important that you reach out to the state you are forming your entity in and find out their requirements and available options.

Some examples of business entities include the following:

1. SOLE PROPRIETORSHIP

This entity is viewed as the easiest to form. A sole proprietorship does not require any formal procedures to initiate and has minimal accounting requirements for set up. You do not need any additional or separate tax forms for this entity because it is done on your own personal income tax returns. With this type of set up, you can exchange business and personal assets freely and without concern.

One of the pros of this type of entity includes quick set up and the ability to share assets between business and personal accounts. One of the cons is that due to the ease of set up and lack of separation of business and personal assets, your personal assets are at much greater risk if lawsuits and liability for personal debts arise. This allows for no shielding of personal assets. This also limits the amount and number of expenses you can write off due to the reporting requirements and capitation that exist for personal tax returns. In this type of set up, you lose out on many favorable deductions which can help decrease your effective tax burden and thus limit your utilization of the revenue you have generated.

2. PARTNERSHIP

This entity is also viewed as a simple entity to form. A partnership functions as what is called a pass-through entity, meaning income and deductions are passed along from the partnership to the individual partners of the entity based on the percentage of ownership or partnership agreed upon between the partners based on the contract signed. Once this occurs, similar to a sole proprietorship, the deductions and income are reported on the personal income tax return of each partner. The partnership itself does not pay taxes thus leaving the tax liability to the individual partners.

One of the pros of this type of entity includes quick set up and the ability to share assets between business and personal accounts. One of the cons is that due to the ease of set up and lack of separation of business and personal assets, your personal assets are at much greater risk if lawsuits and liability for personal debts arise. This allows for no shielding of personal assets. This also limits the amount and number of expenses you can write off due to the reporting requirements and capitation that exist for personal tax returns. In this type of set up, you lose out on many favorable deductions which can help decrease your effective tax burden and thus limit your utilization of the revenue you have generated.

3. LIMITED LIABILITY PARTNERSHIP

Similarities exist between a general partnership and a limited liability partnership (LLP). A big difference between the two entities is that in most states, an LLP may register with the Department of State. This allows for a layer of insulation from liabilities because each partner is exempt from liability for obligations and liabilities arising from the "negligence, omissions, malpractice, wrongful acts, or misconduct" of the other partners.

It is similar to a partnership in that it is also treated as a pass-through entity for federal and state tax purposes. In this capacity, income and losses pass through to the partners either in proportion to ownership or according to your partnership agreement. With this entity, some liability exists, meaning you do not have full protection from liability. You are still open to unlimited personal liability as they pertain to contractual obligations of the partnership. This can come in the form of promissory notes, etc.

4. LIMITED LIABILITY COMPANY

One of the best-known entities is the limited liability company (LLC). This entity provides some flexibility regarding liability protection and taxation. With this entity, you gain the liability protection of a C corporation and have the option of being taxed as a partnership or as a corporation. You are allowed the ability to structure your entity in such a way that you can have unlimited members. Most people find this entity easy to operate. This entity allows for growth and expansion.

You must have an operating agreement that details how you will manage your business. This is an important document as it is requested by banks, mortgage companies, and other institutions as they review your application for loans or setting up bank and other accounts. With this document you can delineate the "control" of the entity and limit where the interest is concentrated.

This entity is desirable due to the fact that it functions as a pass-through for tax purposes but gives the added benefit of limiting your liability similar to that afforded by forming a C corporation. For example, if you are diligent and are able to keep your business assets completely separate from your personal assets, then you are able to limit your liability to business assets.

5. S CORPORATION

The S corporation carries some similarities to that of a C corporation in that it is taxed like a partnership. It is stricter in that it has very specific and well-defined limits of its structure including the number and types of shareholders. This entity has become a favorite of smaller or more closely held entities. Its ability to divide up distributions to shareholders and reclassify those distributions is viewed as a very attractive and desirable feature.

6. C CORPORATION

This entity is what most people think of when they hear the word corporation. Their names usually end with "Inc." The pros of this entity include the following benefits: continuous life, clear divisibility of assets between personal and corporate, limited liability among share-holders, freely transferable shares of stock, virtually unlimited options on structuring stock ownership, and favorable tax treatment for certain expenses.

The cons of this entity include subjection to an increased administrative expense, compliance formalities, and the potential for "double taxation." Things become more complicated with this entity due to more complicated accounting and tax compliance including the need to file corporate returns. You are also placed at the risk of "double taxation" because the entity is a separate taxable entity and does not qualify for pass-through status. As a result, the C corporation pays a tax on its income for the corporate year, and the shareholders pay taxes on dividends received from the corporation. An additional layer exists as the salary, which is paid to FICA for both the employer and employee as it has to be reported as income if the entity is owned by a single person.

CHAPTER 2

MEDICAL LICENSURE

To obtain medical licensure, you must meet certain requirements including obtaining a professional medical degree from an accredited Allopathic or Osteopathic School of Medicine. You must also complete a residency training program. You must pass multiple steps of the United States Medical Licensing Examination (USMLE) and graduate from an accredited medical school. Furthermore, you must complete post-graduate training. You must also apply for licensure in the state in which you plan to practice.

Each state medical licensing board has specific requirements, which need to be met to successfully gain licensure. You will want to contact the state licensing board to obtain a copy of its current licensing requirements. Some states have limits regarding the number of attempts at successful completion of the licensing exam.

They may also have time limits for completing the licensing examination sequence.

Some states have additional requirements before you can successfully obtain licensure. In some states, this includes additional exams, completion of topic-specific coursework, criminal background check, participation in face-to-face interviews, proof of participation in training programs and/or a log of continuing medical education courses. For example, Texas and Nevada require you to pass the jurisprudence exam. It is important to know which states require additional testing, so you can prepare to successfully pass the exam.

Most states require you to maintain a medical license in good standing to practice within the state. Each state has its own rules and regulations that govern how to maintain a medical license in good standing. This is different from maintenance of board certification. Most states require renewal of licensure at least yearly. It is important to maintain a license in good standing to preserve the ability to practice.

The timeframe for obtaining a medical license differs from state to state and during the time of year you apply. Expect delays when applying for licensure leading up to the start of residency in July of each year. You can obtain a list of typical wait times by contacting the state medical board for which you are applying. Another factor that can impact timeframe for obtaining licensure includes the response time of medical school or postgraduate training programs. The application file itself and its complexity may prolong the timeframe in which the license is granted. Resources do exist for expediting or simplifying the licensure process. Recently, formation of an Interstate Licensing Commission has streamlined the process for the states that participate in this commission. This has served to ease the process for physicians looking to practice in these states.

CHAPTER 3

MALPRACTICE

Factors to consider prior to purchasing medical malpractice insurance include the state or location in which you wish to practice and your medical specialty. The cost of medical malpractice can drastically differ from state to state and depending on the medical specialty in which you practice. You will want to do extensive research prior to obtaining a policy to get a better idea of the cost associated with securing a policy. For example, specialties that incur higher costs to be insured include orthopedic surgery, neurosurgery, and obstetrics and gynecology. Cost can be influenced by how states award judgments in favor of the patient. States that are known for dispensing higher awards usually have policies, which carry a higher premium.

Other factors that can impact malpractice insurance costs include:

- Your claims history: Medical professionals with fewer claims typically pay lower premiums for malpractice insurance; this favors practitioners fresh out of training.

- Your hours: Long hours means more patients, and that increases your risk of making a mistake; reducing your work week to 20 hours can lower your premiums.

- The size of your practice: The bigger your practice, in terms of both the number of patients and facilities, the higher your costs. This can also be impacted by site of practice. Practitioners that see a higher volume of patients in the skilled nursing setting may incur a higher premium due to the increased risk and exposure.

- Policy limits: You can opt for lower limits if state law allows it but be careful; this means you have less coverage and may be underinsured. Most hospitals require a certain amount of coverage, which may impact this decision.

- Deductibles: Typically, a higher deductible lowers your medical malpractice costs; this may be a good idea for physicians who have enough cash reserves to pay more out of pocket legal costs.

The most common malpractice allegations are:

- Missing or delayed diagnosis
- Negligent prenatal care
- Negligence during childbirth
- Medication errors
- Anesthesia errors
- Surgery errors

Malpractice claims typically focus on a death or serious injury. The following list provides an idea of some of the top reasons why a malpractice claim was filed:

- Death — 31%
- Significant permanent injury — 19%

- Major permanent injury — 18%
- Quadriplegic or brain damaged — 12%
- Minor permanent injury — 8%
- Major temporary injury — 7%
- Minor temporary injury — 3%
- Emotional injury — 1%
- Insignificant injury — 0.4%

You want to obtain a malpractice policy to provide coverage against litigation which may occur during the course of your medical practice. It protects the physician against claims of negligence. Most hospitals and other facilities in which patient contact occurs require this type of coverage. Coverage requirements and limits differ based on state. It is important to thoroughly research the providers in your practice and cross-reference the requirements for your particular sites of practice.

When choosing a policy, you want to avoid the following mistake:

A major mistake is not having a full understanding of the language within the policy.

It is important to have a healthcare lawyer review the terms and language of your medical malpractice insurance policy to make sure you have as robust of a plan as possible. This will shelter you as much as possible from any future claims. This will also prevent you from having to pay many thousands of dollars in unwanted premiums.

If you are unclear when reviewing your policy, please seek clarity regarding the following terms:

- Admitted Carrier: An admitted carrier is an insurance company licensed and regulated by your state department of insurance. When you are insured through an admitted carrier, you are protected by your state's guarantee fund. This means that you are protected in the event your insurer unexpectedly declares bankruptcy, and you have an open claim.

- Annual Aggregate Limit: For a claims-made policy, this number refers to the maximum dollar amount the carrier will pay during the year. This includes all covered claims, which means your aggregate limit is greatly reduced if you have multiple cases to settle at one time.

- Consent to Settle Clause: This clause states that your insurance carrier can't settle a claim without your written consent. If your policy doesn't contain this clause, you run the risk of your carrier settling a claim that has no merit simply because the settlement is less costly than a full defense.

To obtain as much clarity as possible, you want to inquire about the complete details of your policy. You want to obtain a complete copy of your malpractice insurance policy and all applicable endorsements for your records. Read these documents carefully and have them reviewed by a healthcare lawyer to provide clarity on the terms and stipulations you are not familiar with.

If you perform procedures in your practice, you want to verify the procedures you perform are covered under the policy you are looking to obtain. You must fully disclose all procedures and areas of risk in your practice to avoid denial of coverage or a cancellation of your policy for failing to disclose a certain procedure or added exposure or risk.

You want to be aware of any policy exclusions such as issues relating to libel, slander, sexual misconduct, or criminal acts. Issues related to fee disputes are usually not covered since they are considered a contract issue as opposed to a valid malpractice claim. Your policy may also exclude services performed on a voluntary basis or have territorial restrictions that limit your ability to see patients who are visiting from another state.

It is important to consider potential exclusions of coverage due to conduct that is not covered, defense, settlement, and tail coverage. Tail coverage protects against claims that occur for a certain time period after terminating a claims-based or claims-paid policy. This type of coverage is also useful for those who cannot obtain nose coverage. Protecting yourself from liability is important in maintaining a profitable practice. Some hospital by-laws also require coverage for future claims even after they have left a practice.

Policies are specific to the state in which you practice. Certain states require different amounts of coverage. It is important to research and state specific requirements before securing a policy. Each state has a statute of limitations by which a claim must be filed. Some states have placed a limit or cap on the amount of damages that is paid out for a claim.

Types of policies to consider include claims-based versus occurrence-based. Claims-based policies cover incidents which occurred during the time period the policy was valid and in place, as well as when the alleged act occurred if this was within the time period when the policy was valid and in place. An occurrence-based policy will cover the policyholder during the time the policy was valid and in place regardless of when the claim was initially filed.

Each policy has a coverage limit. A coverage limit is the amount of money that will be paid out for each claim. It is important to research the coverage limit for the state in which you plan to practice. You will need to discuss these limit requirements with the insurer to verify you have the proper coverage requirements. Certain hospitals will also designate requirements of coverage to obtain staff privileges. An example of a typical coverage requirement would be obtaining a policy of $1,000,000/$3,000,000 which provides a maximum of $1M per claim and $3M for all claims during a policy term.

Some other types of policy considerations that may shield you from a lawsuit include the following:

- Cyber Liability Coverage: This coverage protects you against liability due to technical issues like data being compromised by a disgruntled employee, security breaches caused by hackers, virus-related problems, or identity theft. It can also provide protection against liability relating to HIPAA or HITECH Act violations.

- First Dollar Coverage: This means you have no deductible and zero out-of-pocket expenses relating to a claim.

- Hammer Clause: A hammer clause forces you to comply with your carrier's decision to settle a claim regardless of its merit. If you refuse to settle, you're responsible for any costs incurred above the settlement amount. For example, if the plaintiff in a case wants $75,000 to settle a claim and you refuse to accept the offer despite your carrier's request to do so, you're personally liable for any judgment awarded in excess of the $75,000 when the case goes to trial. Ignoring a hammer clause opens you up to serious financial risk.

- Locum Tenens Coverage: This type of coverage lets you use a substitute physician to temporarily perform your duties without affecting your coverage as long as the carrier is properly notified of the physician's name and dates in which he or she will be assuming your duties. Locum tenens means "place holder" — indicating that the physician is only filling in due to vacation, illness, or sabbatical.

- Non-admitted Carrier: A non-admitted carrier is an insurance company that is not licensed or regulated by your state department of insurance. When you are insured through a non-admitted carrier, you lack the protection of being covered by your state's guarantee fund. However, a non-admitted carrier can be a viable option if you require excess and surplus lines coverage.

CHAPTER 4

BILLING COMPANY

Choosing the correct billing company is an important step in maximizing your revenue.

You want a billing company that makes the least amount of errors, as you want a company that will help you collect every dollar you generate.

The goal is to choose a company with a solid reputation in the market and that has proven results. It is important to do market research when considering a billing company. One important factor to consider includes the percentage of collections. The goal is to keep the highest percentage of collections possible while collecting as much revenue as possible. Prior to hiring any billing company, you want to check to ensure they do not employ any individuals that may have been excluded from a federal program or have been placed on a Medicare exclusion list.

You want to choose a billing company that employs staff members who are certified by the American Medical Billing Association (AMBA). You want to find out whether the staff has obtained a Medical Reimbursement Specialist certification.

This certification implies that the recipient is knowledgeable in the areas of:

- ICD-10, CPT4 and HCPCS coding;
- Medical terminology;
- Insurance claims and billing, appeals and denials, fraud and abuse;
- HIPAA and Office of Inspector General (OIG) compliance;
- Information and web technology; and,
- Reimbursement.

When considering which billing company to choose you want to first consider the type of billing company you will feel most comfortable with. In general, three types of billing companies exist. These include the following types:

- **Small-scale Medical Billing Services**

  These can be considered mom and pop billing companies in that they are usually operated out of the home of the individual doing the billing. These are tailored to practices that have a limited budget and see a smaller/lower volume of patient encounters. With this type of practice and any other, you want to ensure they have sufficient experience in healthcare billing.

- **Professional Medical Billing Business**

  These are considered a huge step up from the small-scale services in that they can handle a larger volume and provide additional services which the smaller-scale companies can not provide. They also require a larger portion of your budget to secure their services. You will need to inquire about the additional services they can provide that are available to you.

- **Physician Practice Management Company**

  These can be considered the behemoths of the billing companies. These companies typically have upwards of 200 staff members and have a very robust and well-equipped infrastructure. Due to their ability and capacity, they will require a very large portion of your budget to secure their services. They provide full service management of your practice assuming responsibility for almost all aspects of your billing.

When choosing a billing company, you want to consider pricing options. Generally, three pricing options exist. Percentage-based pricing occurs when the service is charged based on a percentage of collections or a percentage of gross claims submitted or total collections. The benefit of this model is that the success of the billing company is tied to the success of the practice, which means they have an incentive for you to be successful. One pitfall of these billing companies is that small claims may not be pursued as aggressively as other claims due to lower payoff, meaning the possibility of losing out on funds exists although this may be a small amount of revenue.

A fee-based model is based on the billing company charging a fixed dollar amount per claim submitted. The benefit for this model is that it may be more cost effective. The pitfall is that there is less incentive for the billing company to follow up on denied claims thus creating a possibility of lost revenue.

A hybrid model exists in which the billing company charges on a percentage basis for certain carriers or balances and charges a flat fee for others. The benefit of this model is that it may be more cost effective. The pitfall is that there is less incentive to follow up on certain claims again creating the possibility of lost revenue. Of all three models, the percentage-based model is the most common.

You want to inquire about whether the billing company will be able to provide assistance in complying with PQRI reporting data and Meaningful Use reports.

It is important to have the billing company provide clarity on the onboarding process. You want clarity as to whether there are any technical resources your practice would require in order to hand over the billing operations to them. You want to know an estimate of the setup time, when you can expect to be fully operational, and any technical requirements that may require systems upgrades on your part.

You also want to get clarity regarding what specific services will be included in the percentage per month you are paying. For example, will credentialing with the insurance carriers be included in this percentage? Will they provide hospital credentialing as a part of the monthly percentage? Will you be charged additional clearinghouse fees, or will these be included? You want clarity regarding whether or not the percentage you are charged covers collection of co-pays.

You want to know how responsive the billing company will be regarding billing and coding issues. You want them to have a robust and capable customer support team that can handle your issues promptly.

When considering a billing company, you want to consider the following questions:

- How many people will be assigned to my account?

- How many years of experience do they have in billing?

- How much experience do they have in my specialty?

- How do you ensure your billers are kept up to date on codes and regulations?

- What are your average days in accounts receivable for my specialty?

- What percentage of charges are turned over to a collection agency?

- What type of insurance coverage do you carry? (Errors and omission coverage? Liability for security breaches?)

You want to ask if the billing company utilizes a cloud-based system that offers 24/7 access to any claim in the queue and any data point you need. You want to have access to (number of claims denied, days in AR, etc.) You will also want to be provided with reconciliation reports showing charges, payments, write-offs, adjustments, open charges, unapplied payments, and posted payments – broken down by user, provider, legal entity, location, and payer. You want to be provided with a report of unbilled superbills, superbills on hold, flagged superbills, and charges on hold.

Standard reports you should expect to be provided with should include the following reports:

- Charges Summary
- Payments Summary
- Aging Summary (A/R)
- Aging Claims (by insurer)
- Adjustments Summary (write-offs, refunds)
- Visits
- Procedures

– Denials

– Collections activity report

When considering companies, you want to fig-ure out what percentage of collections they take and how successful they are at collecting as much revenue as possible from the primary insurance and any secondary, tertiary, or other carriers the patient has. The processing of car-riers other than the primary insurance will serve as a source of additional revenue, which boosts your collections. These claims are sub-mitted and cover the amount of funds, which remain after the primary insurance has paid out for services rendered. This can be a huge fi-nancial windfall for a practice if done correctly. You want to also consider how effective they are with processing worker's compensation claims.

You want to know exactly how the company will pursue denied claims. You want to find out whether or not they will pursue the claims or if this responsibility is left to you the provider. You want to have an idea of what the process is for handling a denied claim and how the pro-vider can hold them accountable for fully pursuing and processing the claim to completion and resolution.

You want clarity on how the billing company will follow up on unpaid claims. You want to know what occurs if a patient does not pay their bill. You want clarity on how the billing company will conduct follow up on this unpaid claim. You want to ensure the billing company follows and complies with all regulations regarding handling and processing patient information. You want to make sure the billing company has a plan and policy in place to protect patient privacy.

You want to make sure the company has a robust system to provide financial reports and statements, so you can track your revenue in real time. You want them to have the ability to break down your revenue in multiple ways. You want to see what amount of revenue the 30-day, 60-day, 90-day, and greater than 90-day account receivables generated. You want to be able to see reports by payer. You want to be able to see reports by patient, date of service, as well as on a daily, weekly, monthly, and yearly basis.

You want your billing company to be responsive in a timely fashion regarding any billing or revenue concerns that may arise. You want them to have a system for receiving non-electronic payments and depositing them into your business account timely. You want them to perform credentialing at minimal to no extra cost. You want them to perform at least quarterly audits of billing to ensure you remain in compliance and that your documentation justifies the level of billing you are conducting. Issues to address prior to signing a contractual agreement include how the billing company will handle delays in claim generation, irregular follow-ups, and accountability.

You want to understand the percentage of Medicare they carry and how that relates to the percentage of charges they collect. The percentage of Medicare they are charging will impact the percentage of collections you will expect. This is important as this helps determine if the company is collecting the highest possible percentage of revenue you are generating. Typically, you would expect a company to collect 50-60 percent of what they are charging. You want to verify any additional costs outside of processing claims and collecting revenue. You want to verify whether they are charging a percentage based on gross collections or net collections as gross collections may not be an accurate representation of the revenue you expect to bring in. You also want the company to have a short period of time in which the funds are in receivables outstanding as this reflects how well and efficiently the company is processing claims.

You want to know how your billing company utilizes technology in the processing of your claims. You want to seek clarity regarding how the company conducts its information sharing, data security, recovery procedures, and data backup procedures.

They must address the following potential technological issues:

- How will superbills and claims be shared?

- How does the billing service fit with the provider's electronic health record (EHR) strategy?

- Does the service have an integrated EHR?
- How does the service ensure data security?
- What are the disaster recovery procedures?
- Where and how is backup data stored?
- Will a provider need to install and maintain software or access the system online?
- Is the technology HIPAA-compliant?

You want to find out if the billing company employs technology that can integrate with the provider's EMR. You want to inquire about whether the billing company uses artificial intelligence to develop smart rules-based software that checks the claims before filing. This is important because the use of artificial intelligence can significantly reduce the risk of inaccurate claims being processed and reduce denials and help increase the percentage of clean claims being processed the first time around. This helps to get you paid early and reduces unforeseen revenue loss.

CHAPTER 5

ACCOUNTANT

It is important to find a good accountant. Tips on finding a good accountant include seeking referrals from your attorney, business banker, or a close colleague. Other options for finding a good accountant include researching the Society of Certified Public Accountants for the state in which you plan to practice. After obtaining a name, you will need to interview candidates and focus on specific questions related to your practice needs.

Your accountant's services can be broken up into a few categories including management of transactions and creating and processing returns and financial statements. You will need to interview your potential candidates, focusing on examining which services they will provide, personality fit for your needs, and the fees they will charge for the services rendered.

You will want to know what services your accountant will provide including tax processing, auditing, and bookkeeping services. Another service to inquire about is estate planning. You want to get a feel for the personality and practice style of the accountant. You want to try to ascertain whether they lean toward a more conservative approach versus a more aggressive approach when filing your taxes. You want to obtain clarity on the fees you will be charged for the services they provide. You want clarity on whether they charge a monthly retainer versus an hourly rate. You want to assess the potential yearly charges based on the amount of work you anticipate they will perform.

It is very important to choose an accountant who understands your financial goals and possesses a similar philosophy regarding risk and aggression. You want to verify all credentials and degrees claimed by the individual. You want to do market research, and if possible, contact current and former clients to get reviews of his or her work. You want an accountant who is knowledgeable and can minimize your effective tax burden while functioning within the rules of the law. Your accountant will need to understand what you want to achieve financially in the short, intermediate, and long-term. Your accountant will need to be open and willing to communicate intimately with your team, including your financial planner, business banker, and tax lawyer. You will need to gauge his or her level of aggression and verify your comfort with that level.

You want to research and gauge your accountant's mastery of current tax law and strategies for maximizing revenue within the limits of these laws. You want to verify that your accountant checks with the state in which you practice to discover any tax laws that have been altered along with any updates to tax forms. You want to check with the accountant to see if they are members of or subscribe to the American Institute of CPAs weekly newsletter to keep abreast of updates and changes to the tax law. You want your accountant to have the ability to maximize your revenue and decrease your effective tax burden as much as possible.

You want your accountant to effectively communicate with your financial planner to execute your financial strategy and vision. You want someone who is open and available to discuss financial planning as it relates to your tax obligations and retirement planning. You want your accountant to work in concert with the entire financial team you created in order to achieve optimal results and maximize the revenue you generate. You want your financial planner and accountant to have a direct line to each other, so they can align and execute your financial vision.

You want your accountant to aid in connecting you to other resources, which will help grow your business. You want your accountant to be available to discuss all further practice grow and changes with your financial planner to ensure you remain on track to achieve the financial goals you set forth. You want your accountant to understand the implications of your retirement accounts on your tax liabilities.

CHAPTER 6

FINANCIAL PLANNER

When searching for a financial planner, it is important to understand the definition of fiduciary because it has a tremendous impact on how your funds are managed. By definition, a fiduciary is an individual or organization that manages assets on behalf of another person or entity. It is assumed that the fiduciary will cultivate a relationship of trust with their client and uphold the fiduciary duty. The fiduciary duty is an ethical obligation to act solely in someone else's best interest. All investment advisors registered with the SEC or a state securities regulator must act as fiduciaries. When searching for a financial planner who is a fiduciary, you can utilize a few resources to help you in your search. These include the National Association of Personal Financial Advisors (NAPFA), which has an online search tool that simplifies the process for finding certified financial planners in your vicinity. If you locate someone using this search tool, you can be assured the advisor operates on a fee-only basis and promises to act as a fiduciary. Another option available in your search is the Garrett Planning Network, which is an organization of fiduciary financial planners who charge an hourly rate. You can also conduct a search using a tool provided by the Certified Financial Planners Board. The site also allows you to look into the planner's experience and history. Once you settle on an advisor, you should seek clarity about how the advisor earns money, what certifications and licenses they hold, what services they offer, who is a typical client, how often they communicate with you, and if they can provide a written guarantee of their fiduciary duty. Obtaining a copy of the advisor's SEC-filed paperwork is important because it gives you the ability to verify the advisor's business, pay structure, educational background, potential conflicts of interest, and disciplinary history.

You want to find and hire a financial planner who has a fiduciary duty while managing your financial planning. By functioning in that capacity, they are required to manage your assets while acting solely in your best interest. This duty helps to decrease the chance of there being conflicts of interest and builds a level of trust. The fiduciary duty helps to place your mind at ease and allows for more candid discussions as it relates to achieving your financial goals.

Very similar to your accountant you want a financial planner who understands your financial goals and has a similar philosophy regarding risk and aggression. Again, similar to your accountant, you want to verify all credentials and degrees claimed by the individual. You want to do market research, and if possible, contact current and former clients to get reviews about their work. You want a financial planner who is knowledgeable about all vehicles and strategies available to help maximize wealth and prosperity for future generations. Your financial planner will need to understand what you want to achieve financially in the short, intermediate, and long-term. Your financial planner will need to be open and willing to communicate intimately with your team, which will include your accountant, business banker, and tax lawyer. You will need to gauge his or her level of aggression and verify your comfort with that level.

Your financial planner will need to work closely with you and your financial team to help you understand your finances and financial circumstances. They will need to have an intimate understanding of your total annual income, debt obligations, monthly expenses not related to debt, current investment holdings, savings account balances, tax liabilities, and insurance plans. After undertaking an in-depth analysis, he or she will need to work with you and your financial team to develop a strategy to achieve your financial goals.

Your financial planner will need to have a good understanding of your debt to income ratio and discuss debt management strategies. They will need to understand your pattern of savings and savings habits and your budgeting habits and gain a realistic view of your current and planned future budgeting. They will also need to gain insight into what you want to do regarding investment strategies, estate planning, and utilization of insurance as a method of saving, and retirement funds allocation. They will need to understand how this all relates to your financial goals.

Your financial planner will need to work with your accountant to assist in providing the best tax efficiency strategies. They will need to have a good understanding of your cash flow, projected revenue, debt management corporate structure, and any future plans for expansion of your workforce. They will need to understand future growth to help orchestrate your financial future.

CHAPTER 7

BUSINESS BANKER

When choosing your business banker, first you want to consider whether they function within a large or small bank. One other factor to consider is whether there is convenient access to funds; this comes in the form of easily accessible ATMs and extended walk up hours. Also, some banking institutions have more locations and presence in certain areas of the country compared to others. You want to consider the fees associated with holding and accessing your money. In comparison to larger banks, smaller banks have lower fees. You want to consider the type of service you will be provided. The product line offered by a smaller institution may dwarf those offered by a larger institution but may be limited by the speed at which they can conduct business in general.

Your business banker will need to work closely with you and your financial team to help you understand your finances and financial circumstances. Your banker will assist you in developing effective relationships in the community and help you grow your business. Your business banker will assist you in reviewing your portfolio and assist with engaging in new business acquisitions. Your business banker will assist in securing business loans and financial products that help you grow. Your business banker will help you to obtain and manage a business line of credit and maintain credit quality.

Your business banker will help you develop a small business plan, which meets the financial plan laid out by you and your financial team. They help to make sure when transactions are conducted they are done within all compliance standards and policies to make sure it is a secure transaction. Your business banker will assist in managing your communication with the bank staff. Your business banker is in charge of maintaining customer satisfaction and excellent customer service.

Your business banker will help you with the financing you will need to expand your business, conduct acquisitions as you grow, purchase equipment as you expand, and assist with funding operating expenses. They can assist you in obtaining various loans to expand and grow your practice. They will serve as your financial bridge to the community.

Your business banker will serve as your financial lifeline as you build and grow your business. Their access and connections in the community will help you connect with the resources you need for sustained growth. Your business banker will help to secure access to credit which can be utilized for growth related purchases. Your business banker can connect you with the local chamber of commerce to help increase your exposure in your local market. Your business banker is a key component in the financial team you develop and must be open to communicating with the other members of your financial team.

Your business banker can help connect you with local resources in the community and help secure funding for start-up and growth. Your business banker will monitor and track the daily financial transactions to monitor trends.

They will review bank statements, loan applications, and other financial documents to monitor and alert you about any suspicious or fraudulent activity. They will assist in creating a documentation system to organize your financial documents.

CHAPTER 8

LAWYER

You will need a good lawyer to assist with managing any legal matters, which your business may encounter during its lifetime. They can assist in obtaining copyrights and trademarks and advise you on business incorporation, lawsuits, and liability. A lawyer can assist with handling any lawsuit. They will work in conjunction with your business team to draft and execute contracts, form business organizations, file taxes, and apply for licensing. Your lawyer will need to communicate with your accountant, financial planner, and business banker to ensure proper coordination and business set-up.

One thing to consider when choosing a lawyer is whether they work for a large firm versus a small firm. The size of the firm may impact the fees and the amount you pay for services rendered. There are pros and cons to each. First, large firms have more resources available to assist with multiple tasks at once and have multiple staff members available in house. Secondly, they have more leverage on a local, regional, and sometimes national scale, which may translate into future connections, leading to expedited growth.

You will need to consider and discuss the fee structure of the lawyer you wish to obtain. Some options available include flat-fee, retainer, hourly, per diem, contingency, and value billing is available sometimes. Each fee structure carries its own pros and cons, which you will need to discuss with your accountant. For simple matters, flat-fee pricing is an ideal approach and can minimize costs. During the initial start-up of your business, it may be most ideal to function on a retainer basis due to the large volume of questions that will need to be answered.

You will need to be aware of the different types of lawyers available and the areas they specialize in. You want a lawyer who has knowledge of different topics, while specializing in business law. You want to gauge their level of experience, length of practice, connections to other industries, whether or not they have other clients in your field or business, practice style, and whether they are open to different billing options.

Your lawyer will need to be able to assist with contracts, business organization, taxes, and licensing. Keep in mind that as your business grows, you may be faced with issues regarding intellectual property and may need your lawyer to assist. It is important to gauge your lawyer's comfort level with this, and if he or she is not comfortable with their ability in certain areas, they should be able to refer you to a specialist in that area. Your lawyer is a key component to making sure the legal foundation of your business is solid. Your lawyer will set the tone for the level of risk your business is faced with.

CHAPTER 9

INSURANCE BROKER

You will need to research and find an insurance broker. A broker differs from an insurance agent in that the broker has a duty to work in your best interest where as an insurance agent works on behalf of an insurance company. The state specific governing body in which they work regulates brokers. They must obtain an insurance broker license and pass an exam. They must also submit to fingerprinting and a background check.

Your insurance broker will assist you in obtaining the best coverage for your specific needs. They can assist you in making a claim. They will assist and help you find the best conditions and rates. Your broker will work directly with you to help navigate the insurance landscape and obtain the best deal possible. They will also look to consolidate coverage when possible to give you the best product possible, which provides the most robust amount of coverage.

Your broker will assist you in obtaining health insurance, including dental and vision plans. Due to their expertise, they will help assess the cost/benefit ratio when obtaining an individual versus a group health insurance plan. They will help you analyze what is best for your practice and financial goals while helping you to obtain maximum coverage to protect you. Once you have decided on a plan, they will work on your behalf to obtain the best rates. They will also need to communicate with your financial team to ensure all financial or investment implications are considered.

Your broker may also assist you in obtaining auto insurance.

CHAPTER 10

PRACTICE SETTING

You will need to consider the different practice settings and the billing and coding implications that come along with them. You will need to ensure you are billing the correct codes for the particular setting in which you practice. You will need to understand the nuances each setting presents. You will need to understand what requirements are needed to bill in that particular setting. You will also need to have an understanding of when and where patients can be seen.

Different potential practice settings include the acute care hospital. In this setting, you function as a consultant and content expert to determine the appropriate level of care and aid in disposition. You work in conjunction with the therapy team along with providing both medical and functional expertise to assist in transitioning patients to the most appropriate level of care. In your role, you are ideally trained to assist in transitioning the patient through the post-acute care continuum. You are the content expert that assists in decreasing length of stay and readmissions.

In the acute inpatient rehabilitation hospital or rehabilitation unit, you function as the leader of the interdisciplinary team. You oversee the functional progress of the patients as they embark upon their rehabilitation journey. You lead and conduct the weekly interdisciplinary team meeting, helping to assess barriers to discharge, assist in discharge planning, and develop a plan of care to help maximize the patients' function prior to discharge. You direct the therapy team and prescribe modalities and medications to decrease barriers and maximize function. You assist in helping to usher the patients back into society at their peak functional status.

In the subacute or skilled nursing setting, you function in a very similar capacity as that which occurs in the acute rehabilitation setting. You are charged with overseeing the functional progress of the patient, tailoring their therapy program, and helping to maximize function. You participate in and lead the team meeting, facilitating input and determining discharge planning and whether the patient is appropriate to transition to a higher level of care, i.e. acute inpatient rehabilitation or if the patient is safe to discharge home. You help to determine what ongoing therapy needs the patient will most likely have once discharged.

In the long-term acute care hospital setting, you function in a very similar capacity as that which occurs in the subacute or skilled nursing facility. You are charged with overseeing the functional progress of the patient, ensuring they do not develop any complications from immobility including contracture, bedsores, or venous thrombosis. You participate in and lead the team meeting, facilitating input and determining discharge planning and whether the patient is appropriate to transition to a higher level of care, i.e. acute rehab versus skilled nursing. You help to determine the most appropriate level of care and assist with discharge planning.

CHAPTER 11

CPT CODES

You will need to understand CPT (Current Procedural Terminology) codes as they relate to the practice setting in which you are conducting patient visits. You will need to understand the difference between new and existing patients. You will need to understand which modifiers are allowed to be added on to the existing codes you are billing. You will need to know the specific evaluation and management codes that correlate with the visit you are conducting. You will need to understand when and where to bill specific codes.

You will need to understand the requirements for time-based billing versus complexity-based billing. To bill based on time, you will need to document that counseling and/or coordination of care dominated more than 50 percent of the physician/patient and/or family encounter (face-to-face time). To bill based on complexity, you must consider medical complexity and decision-making and document varying exam and review of system findings in conjunction with complex decision-making. All documentation must be justifying the complexity for which you are coding.

You must understand the different CPT codes associated with the different levels of care. In the subacute or skilled nursing level of care, initial consultation codes range from 99304-99306 with 99306 carrying the highest complexity and time spent. For follow-up visits, the codes range from 99307 to 99310 with 99310 carrying the highest complexity and time spent. You will need to understand the documentation requirements for each level of coding to best justify billing the code.

You must understand the different CPT codes associated with the different levels of care in both the acute care hospital and the acute inpatient rehabilitation hospital or unit . The initial consultation codes range from 99221 to 99223 with 99223 carrying the highest complexity and time spent. For follow-up visits, the codes range from 99231 to 99233 with 99233 carrying the highest complexity and time spent. You will need to understand how to best justify billing these levels.

You must understand the different CPT codes associated with the different levels of care in the home setting. The initial consultation codes exist for both new and existing patients and for home versus rest home or domiciliary. The codes range from 99341 to 99345 for new home visits with 99345 carrying the highest complexity and time spent. The codes range from 99347 to 99350 for established home visits with 99350 carrying the highest complexity and time spent. The codes range from 99324 to 99328 for new domiciliary visits with 99328 carrying the highest complexity and time spent. The codes range from 99334 to 99337 for established domiciliary visits with 99337 carrying the highest complexity and time spent.

CHAPTER 12

MEDICARE VERSUS COMMERCIAL

You must understand that Medicare will reimburse 80 percent of the physician fee schedule, leaving the patient with the responsibility of covering the remaining 20 percent. This can potentially be covered by a co-insurance if the patient has coverage. Commercial insurance carriers pay based on an agreed upon fee schedule determined by a contractual agreement the provider signs with the commercial carrier. These rates can sometimes exceed Medicare rates, but they can also be below Medicare rates. Understanding the fee schedule for both Medicare and commercial carriers allows for more certainty regarding expected reimbursement.

Typically, you can expect payment from Medicare 10-14 business days after a claim is filed cleanly. Clean claims are those that have all of the correct insurance and demographic information when the initial claim is submitted. Claims can be submitted either electronically or via paper. Paper claims take longer to process and typically are paid out in a longer time period. Typically, the industry standard is to set up electronic submission and receipt to help expedite the collections process.

When submitting claims for commercial insurance plans, you can expect payment anywhere from 10-30 business days once a claim is filed cleanly. With commercial carriers, claims can sometimes take an extended period of time to pay out which may require the billing company to conduct multiple follow-up calls to help facilitate collection of funds. Again, paper claims take longer to process and typically are paid out in a longer time period. Typically, the industry standard is to set-up electronic submission and receipt to help expedite the collections process.

Once the claims have been completed and all information has been verified, the claim is then submitted to a clearinghouse to be processed. The clearinghouse functions as a go-between with the provider's billing company and the insurance carrier. The clearinghouse functions as a data repository for claims where they are then sorted and subsequently directed on to the specific insurance carrier for final processing. This is done by reviewing the claims for errors, placing the data into a HIPAA-compliant format and then forwarding them to the insurance carrier. The clearinghouse updates the provider's billing company on the status of the claim.

After the claims have been submitted, the insurance carrier reviews the claims. Once this review has occurred, the carrier is responsible for providing both the patient and the physician what is called an Explanation of Benefits (EOB). The EOB serves as a breakdown of the process, which is called adjudication. Adjudication is the process whereby a decision is made to either pay a claim or deny a claim after comparing the claim to the benefit or coverage requirements of the patient. Once this process is complete, they will submit the EOB, which shows the dates of service, procedures and charges, patient financial responsibility, and the amount paid to the physician. The payment to the physician is also submitted at this time if all factors are favorable.

CHAPTER 13

EFFICIENCIES OF PRACTICE

Serious consideration must be given to the ways to make your practice as efficient as possible. You want to take a broad view of your practice to identify any potential areas where you can streamline your day-to-day operations to enable you to see the greatest number of patients in the least amount of time. You will need to review your practice design in great detail and be willing to adjust areas as you identify structural flaws that prevent you from achieving your highest level of efficiency. You will want to examine your electronic medical record (EMR) and how it interfaces with current technology and workflow. You want to find as many areas as possible where your EMR can automate your workflow and streamline charting, chart review, and documentation. You want to decrease your workload as much as possible and operate in the leanest possible manner. You want to explore the use of medical scribes, automated dictation, prepopulated notes and billing systems, which streamline how you bill for services rendered.

You want to look into ways to streamline the patient visit while still maintaining a sense of time spent. Some ways to do this are by applying strategies which make the patient feel you spent a greater amount of time than was actually spent. You want to create ways and situations in which the perception of time spent is inflated by the patient due to the strategy you employ.

You want to streamline your day-to-day medical practice operations first by reviewing the time and technique you use to perform some of the following activities. This will allow you to identify areas of your day, which consume a large amount of time and enable you to assess how to make the process more efficient.

Some potential areas of opportunity include the following:

- Scheduling patient visits
- Collecting patient factsheets

- Physical paperwork
- Billing and coding
- Documentation

When you review how you schedule or conduct patient visits, you will find out that one of the most efficient ways to see a large volume of patients is to ensure the highest number of patients are in their rooms at the same time. This gives you the ability to move from room to room to room and conduct the highest number of patient visits in the shortest amount of time. This may be determined by the therapy schedule and/or any other appointment obligations the patient has. Scheduled mealtimes such as breakfast, lunch, and dinner can impact these times but also serve as benchmarks for when patients can be expected to be in their rooms. In most facilities, patients' therapy will end 30 minutes to an hour prior to a scheduled mealtime. This scheduling quirk will allow you to efficiently time your patient visits and organize them in such a way that you are able to cover a block of rooms in a short period of time. This helps to increase the number of patient encounters you can conduct.

Once you have conducted the highest number of patient encounters in the shortest time possible, the next area of efficiency you want to focus on is that of collecting the factsheets for billing purposes. One of the easiest ways to achieve this is by having the factsheets placed in one folder in an area of your designation to limit time wasted searching charts or having to print factsheets for each patient seen. You can also apply this strategy for any and all paperwork that needs to be signed including x-ray results, home health orders, tube feeding orders, and DME orders. A signature stamp can be helpful in cutting down on the amount of time it takes to sign all the orders and documents that accumulate over the course of the day.

The ability to streamline billing and coding is another area of potential efficiency. You want to develop a system in which you can quickly identify the CPT code and level of complexity of your patient encounter and have that information transferred to your billing company, so they can process the claim as quickly as possible. Some providers have developed a system where they assign a roman numeral or letter and number value to a specific CPT code, so that once this is communicated, the correct code is then transmitted to the billing company so the claim can be processed. For example, a high-level initial evaluation acute care hospital would carry the following symbol and number: A3; this would then be transmitted to the billing company as the CPT 99223. This system can be employed in all practice settings using site specific symbols and numbers to quickly communicate the level of visit and complexity, so information from the patient encounter can be communicated to the billing company and subsequently process the claim as quickly as possible to expedite reimbursement for the services rendered.

The billing process can further be streamlined by developing a system in which the diagnosis codes are sent to the provider and/or the biller/billing company, so they can be added along with the CPT to facilitate submission of a clean claim. An example of a system that may exist is the development of a relationship and rapport with the HIMS/Medical Records department such that immediately after the coding documentation for the current patient encounter is available, this information is immediately transmitted via secure email or fax to the provider/biller/billing company to expedite submission of clean claims. Outsourcing the physical data entry function of entering patient demographics, diagnostic codes, and CPT codes allows the provider to utilize that time engaging in activities that can generate more revenue. The hours spent doing what amounts to clerical work can now be put toward seeing more patients more efficiently and funneling these added encounters into your system, so you are able to maximize your time while generating the most revenue within the shortest possible time.

You want to develop a system of documentation that is streamlined and reproducible. You want to employ the conveyor belt approach as much as possible, so documentation is accurate and provides clinical direction and clarity but does not create such a time burden you are not able to be efficient in conducting the greatest volume of patient encounters possible. Using the SOAP format, you can evaluate ways in which to make your documentation quick, concise, and impactful.

For most encounters, you may be able to use your EMR to assist with streamlining your documentation. Depending on the functionality or your EMR, you may be able to prepopulate your note, so that relevant and impactful information is automatically pulled into the medical record and notes you are creating to document your patient encounter. This may come in the form of having the objective information such as vital signs, recent/current labs, urine input/output, tube feeding data, diagnostic imaging, progress in therapy including PT/OT/Speech notes, current functional status regarding ADLs, and ambulation automatically pulled into the note in designated spots which are readily visible in the well-known SOAP format.

In addition to this, the assessment and plan, along with the physical exam, can be carried over and changed on a daily basis as the status of the patient changes such that an accurate reflection of the patient's physical status, plan of care, and progress in therapy is documented in the most efficient way possible. A section for the subjective can be left blank and filled in daily as this changes along with making the appropriate changes to any objective data as it occurs in real-time.

The use of a scribe can also aid in creating efficiency in the area of documentation. You can develop a brand of shorthand which is communicated to a scribe in short phrases which eliminates the need to dictate long phrases of complex medical jargon. The shorthand will function as a method of communicating what needs to be documented in the least amount of time in the most effective way possible. This will also free you of the burdensome task of medical documentation which, again, allows you more time to see patients in an effective and efficient system which increases the volume of patients you can see while decreasing the amount of time it takes to conduct and document these encounters.

THANK YOU

I would like to sincerely thank each and everyone for their support and well wishes. This includes my family, friends, mentors, coaches, and teachers.

Take this opportunity to educate yourself and get on the path to building your own profitable independent practice.

ABOUT THE AUTHOR

Born and raised in Chicago, Illinois, Dr. Hassan Akinbiyi earned his undergraduate degree from Xavier University in Louisiana and his medical doctorate from Indiana University School of Medicine before completing his residency at Marianjoy Rehabilitation Hospital, a part of Northwestern Medicine.

With over ten years of experience, Dr. Hassan is passionate about not only changing the lives of his patients but also helping physicians understand the business of medicine. Known for his work ethic and business acumen, he has turned his knowledge into bestselling books, award-winning blogs, and online training programs employed in transforming new attendings into independent practice owners who control their financial destinies.

Dr. Hassan is very active in supporting rehabilitative medicine policy initiatives at both the local and national levels, and he serves on local hospital foundation boards. As CEO of Akinbiyi Medical Group, LLC, he founded DrHassanRehab.com, the digital hangout spot where physicians go for practical business tips and real-life strategies to help build their practices.

To learn more, visit
DrHassanRehab.com

CREATING DISTINCTIVE BOOKS
WITH INTENTIONAL RESULTS

We're a collaborative group of creative masterminds
with a mission to produce high-quality books to position
you for monumental success in the marketplace.

Our professional team of writers, editors, designers,
and marketing strategists work closely together to ensure
that every detail of your book is a clear representation
of the message in your writing.

Want to know more?
Write to us at info@publishyourgift.com
or call (888) 949-6228

Discover great books, exclusive offers, and more at
www.PublishYourGift.com

Connect with us on social media

@publishyourgift

CPSIA information can be obtained
at www.ICGtesting.com
Printed in the USA
LVHW032257100220
646447LV00021B/938

9 781644 841549